Just SaySomething Vol. II

Grown Folks

KIMBERLY FRAZIER-BURKLEY
AARON SMITH Jr.
LINDA HART-WASHINGTON
LONI LOVE
SHELBY D. HOWARD Jr.

Say Something Enterprise Publishing
Post Office Box 10323
Rockville, MD 20849

The intention of the author of this book is for entertainment, reflection and connection. The book consists of poems of from multiple Authors. Designed for the reader to connect, reflect, acknowledge and come to know.

CONTENTS

ACKNOWLEDGMENTS

To all the unknown writers who want to become an published Author but stop believing it can or will happen for you. As a writer I know you have a awesome story to tell. I know there are words running around in your head to the point it's hard for you to sleep at night. SaySomething Enterprise Publishing wants to give you your opportunity of publishing your long awaited book. Give the world your skills, your art and let your book be a part of your legacy. SaySomething Enterprise Publishing will help you fulfill your dreams! Do it for YOU!
www.saysomethingent.com

Say Something™

1 DEDICATIONS

Linda L. Hart-Washington

I'd like to thank and acknowledge my Lord and Savior Jesus Christ for the gift, and the avenue to present it.

I dedicate this book to my wonderful mother; Angela Lucille Hart, Who taught me patience, and that being by yourself doesn't necessarily mean you are alone, and by beautiful daughter who has so supportive of my love for writing.

Aaron Smith Jr. also known as Poetic NJustice.
I want to dedicate this book to my mother Vhirgo Hensley, my sister's Joy and Tiffany Smith, my late grandfather Howard McCree, my grandmother Patricia McCree, my step father Carlos Hensley and my nieces and nephews Talaya, Amare, and Domo.

Grown Folks

Loni Ross:
Dedicated to my Family, Friends and Haters......
Taking My 1st Step

To My Family for dealing with me.
To those that have been here without
waiver
and those that have doubted the
persistence.
Here we go....

Kimberly Frazier-Burkley

This book is dedicated to Inspiration for stimulation to do creative work, for the human mind to creative thought or to the making of art. Its creativeness the quality of being stimulated to creative thought or activity, or the manifestation of this. Divine influence the divine guidance and influence on human beings. Thank God fpr Inspiration.

Say Something ™

2 FALLING

Ode to a Fallen Angel……. By SD Howard

It was you that they took sight of.
I'll never leave the delight of.
If there were ever frights of.
Never missing a night of, your presence,
your grace, just that simple little face.

Your aura was simply magnificent and the
time that I spent I hope to never ever
forget, what you meant to me. I'm in a
private lil world with thoughts of only you
telling me each and every time about the
little things to do... I can't help but think I
lost you for some of the things that I brought
you, and for that reason my heart weighs real
heavy.

Totally and completely giving myself to the thought
of just you. You are now all around me and I hope
your proud of me.... I imagine all of the things that
we meant to one another and wouldn't change any
of the thing to be with another.... You were there
for me when I had no one and for that reason alone
I already know the outcome.... You're gonna be next
to me till the end of time... and I just want you to know
that your always on my mind......

I miss you more than anything I've known....... but
from me to you.... You'll never be alone.. I love you

I Decline

Happiness streaming through my soul, So
forbidden,
Melodies making me want to sing out loud in a
crowded room,
Preposterous,
Enamored fascination as I tap my feet like a
disobedient child,
Scandalous....
Why am I smiling so much on the inside,
It's truly making my face crack.
How dare someone with a heart of gold protrude
into my darkness.
Deliverance I asked not, but it seems,
deliverance I got.
I will not go softly into this good night,
Your feelings are wrong, mine are right.
I will not fade easily into the
 bright hallows of love,
You were not sent to me from above,
If so you would have come when I cried for you,
When my heart was dying for you,
When the life in my days was relying upon you,
You should have come.
But Not now.....no, I won't have you now....
Yes I will except your warmth on my face....but
not your soft kiss upon my brow

LONI ROSS

Grown Folks

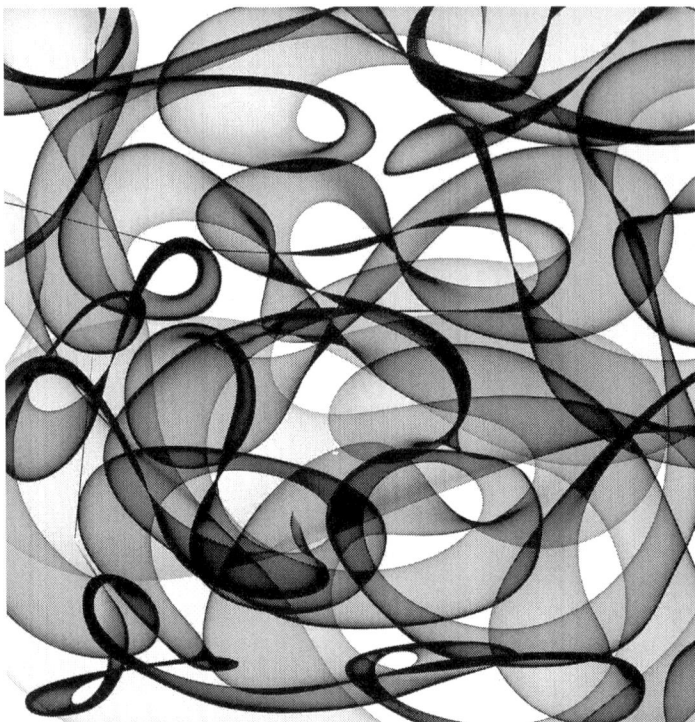

Who U Are Two Me... ... by SD Howard

Emotionally choked by the thoughts that I have of you never being here when I want you to be. Your touch has become that one thing that would allow me to grow in more way than you'll ever know. The way you stroke my face as you take your place and rest completely in my essence and my presence. The softness of your body as you sink into my skin and whisper in my ear about the way that I make you feel.

Taking each second for what its worth and allowing nothing to come into our world...... You mean the world to me and there is never a day that I would allow to pass without me letting you know just that. The scents that omit from your natural glow are enough to let me know that this is it.

I'm drenched in the memories that we have together of what it feels like to be your everything. You are mine and I am yours never will I miss a chance to explore your every want and need in life... You have given me the reason to change my life for you and every season. I'm feeling waters running all over me and I don't want them to stop cause I want to feel your hands as they dry me from head to toe......... and look at your face as you continue to show that wonderful glow.

Grown Folks

<u>Alive</u>

In all the earth and nowhere my flesh has dwelt, seeming to be but not passing through,

I grew up but not out, out of whom I once was, of who I have become, and will remain,

My thoughts haunt me; they chase me in my sleep,

I choose unsuitable paths, paths that never end and lead to nowhere,

Yet every day I make a brand new start, feeling as if I'm somewhere,

But nowhere is where I reside,

The nothingness that surrounds me has grown thick and caused a callus around me,

Everything that I attempt ends up falling to the ground and eventually turning to dust,

There is no moisture so my thoughts just blow away,

The smell of drying flesh is all around me, it has caused the hairs to singe in my nose,

What is the very reason for my existence, and who to ask, for who knows,

The blood in my veins is thick and the flow is slow causing my journey's to be quick and shorter than before,

My skin is cracked and causes much pain and irritation, the process seems to never end,

There's moisture all around me but the callus keeps me bound,

Death reveals itself to me with each breath I take, and in a flash it's gone,

Only to return threatening my life even at my weakest stage,

The colors of life has left me and everything around me is dull,

Another layer has added itself to the already thick callus that's squeezing the life out of me, making it even more difficult to make sense of anything,

People speak to me but it makes no sense, their words are jumbled together and out of context, I cram my eyebrows together and tilt my head in desperation to understand,

And even the light that dwells here is starting to fade, I feel separated from myself,

Like a planet in outer space, few approach me because of the stench of death that consumes my space, even fewer come with a glimmer of hope,

The light that hope brings is only a twinkle through all of the layers,

But just that twinkle pulls me like a magnet, filling me up like water in an empty vessel,

The echo is loud from the sound of emptiness and space,

The water gives way through the cracks in my flesh, causing soothing moisture inside and out, the callus softens and starts to fall away,

The spoken words are much clearer now; the smell of stench has been replaced because of the cleansing, a freshness that caused me to breath again,

I am starting to come to myself and remember who I am and why I belong,

The light is much brighter now, and it's illumination is beautiful, just looking at it fills me, giving me comfort like a baby in it's mothers arms, I feel safe and secure,

The callus has fallen off as the water fills my chest, and I can feel the

Grown Folks

warmth from the light starting to heal my torn skin, I am recovered and life is given back to me,

Love covers me and peace inserts itself in my veins like medicine,

Understanding flows off of others lips like a sweet melody, each note embedding itself in my flesh,

Wisdom lifts her skirt and exposes herself to me, and knowledge escorts a safe passage,

The words drip with honey even as I help myself, filling my belly with its seed to be fertilized so that I'm not alone,

Promises are exposed and recovered even after being dried out, even that whole process couldn't stop what was planted to live to die, my blood is flowing easy again,

Causing my heart to play a selection that was thought to be gone forever,

The chattering has left my teeth alone, and my smile has taken back its rightful place,

The yellow tint that covered my skin now lives with the callus,

And once again I am a reflection of light, life is mine to possess and no darkness can take it away from me, I can only give it away.

Linda Hart - Washington

When Tomorrow's Just a Distant Memory......
By SD Howard

I use to sit around and think of you,

All the lil things we use to do.

All the while there was no substitute for all the things we'd been thru.

I often imagined if you cared about me as much as I did for you.

The things you'd do let me know

That I had no place else to go,

I'm on an emotional rollercoaster and I see no end in sight.

How do I fight?

What a night,

I just think I might have some dynamite

That I want to ignite.....

Blowing this thing right outta the water....

Falling ... Asleep

Pain … Sorrow
Is there a future in tomorrow?

Hate … Envy
Why do these thoughts fight within me?

Greed at high speeds
Why are these traffic lights so green?

With this limitless speed limit
I'm timid to even spit its
a gymnast within my writtens
that keep me from fucking flipping.

Air bags resemble temples
they airheaded to keep life simple.

When I over think it's an etch sketch on my kindle.

I'm trapped in a dream world with beautiful gold
and girls
but my reality is casually casualties that I observe.

See when I dream see I observe the things I feel I
deserve

Grown Folks

the beautiful scene the world at my fingertips I
serve

but the reality is casualties ... the reality of
casualties
so my mentalities a casualty I'm dead to these
bastards see

I battle sleep to cope with beef I'm eager just hope
and dream
cause past accounts have left me weak
and confidence peeks just so it can see
a life without doubt and desert without drought
a moment without withouts
cause fulfillment is only reached when I open my
mouth.

-Aaron Smith aka Poetic NJustice

Thank You for Her Presence... ... by SD Howard

Selfishly I set here with tears streaming down my face. I want to know the reasons why but I know that nothing done by your hands is wrong. My heart feels heavy and just the thought of keeping my family up is an awesome task. I don't think I can make it father, but if this is my assignment please allow me the grace and mercy to do it the way that you would see fit.

I can't believe the road has ended this way, feelings that I didn't get to say things out of my mouth that my sister knew already because of my actions. I can't put into words what Mrs. Debra Crockett(Gibson) meant to the whole of this family unit. We are a loving an selfish family when it comes to the people that are in it and she was the greatest. Father we understand that it was time for your angle to come to be with you and that there is nothing here that would have held here any longer. We just ask that you comfort our minds and hearts and strengthen us in your mighty word as we all seek to get right in your presence. I am speaking solely from my on heart and I don't want to put words out there for anyone else but I just want you all to know what my sister meant to me.

She was the strength when those around her had none.
She was the wisdom when everything around her seemed hopeless.
She was the voice of reason when all sounds around her were
coming from the mouths of fools.

Grown Folks

She was the stability on unstable ground.
She was calming water on a river full of rip tides......
She was a comforter to those that had lost to well to do
for themselves.....
She was a mother to those who had none........
She was it all to those who knew who she was...........
and for that I thank God for allowing her to be in my
life.

I could never have imagined a day without her and now
I have had several and each one of them gets harder
because of all that I see that has happen and the affect
that she had on all that were around her. My sister,
friend, counselor, prayer warrior, supervisor and just
all around everything to me...... Yeah, I know that you
were proud of me but I don't think you really knew
what you truly meant to me....... I miss you so much
Bunch........... and you will always be right there
through it all....

This piece was for my sister-in-law when she passed
away........

<u>SEXY</u>

Your sexy is beautiful to me
Even thou your sexy is skin deep
I'll settle for one shade of gray
If your sexy leads the way
I'll make beauty deep
Hit it hard make it weak
Let sexy put beauty to sleep

KB

I stand behind the tree and watch as you illuminate the
earth,
Never have I been so moved that I would stop my
mating search,
Sit behind the bushes,
And stalk you like you were the most magnificent prey.
Naturally when discovered ....you pushed me away,
and I don't blame you....I was acting like a fool..
A fool in love.
And when you turned to another,
venom raced through my veins,
I blamed you not...for he must be insane.
You were just a token in his sick, twisted game.
So innocent and pure, you knew not what you were,
his puppet, his abuse, his public display whore,
And though you say he never hurt you and treated you
with the utmost respect,
It was I, whom had to stop him,
It was I, forced to slip noose around his neck,
It was I, who lifted his feet of the ground,
and It was I who was forced to hear his last gasp.
See we couldn't be together until it was he who had left,
And though you cried a thousand days and a thousand
nights,
It was only I who could shelter you,
It was only I who could give you light,
Don't run from me,
Don't you dare hide!
I wouldn't harm you like the police said I might,
I just wanna be with you,
In death maybe, if I can't be with you now in life.

LONI ROSS

Going Against The Current

The rushing waters broke the dead silence that covered my ears. I stood there in the hot sun sweating and looking at the water running downstream. The water was running so smooth that it sounded like a familiar tune. I was so tired from traveling I just wanted to rest. Then a small still voice said, "Go upstream". But everyone and everything else is going downstream I said in protest. Plus the current was helping them along the way. Then the voice said, "Get in the water and go against the current, for I have something to give you, besides everything that's easy isn't always rewarding". I stood there for awhile watching a lot of familiar faces and possessions go by. The voice that spoke to me earlier was now gently nudging me towards the water. I was reluctant because I was afraid that I might drown in the rushing water because I was so tired from the long journey. When I stepped in the water I was surprised at feeling instantly revived, what an unusual feeling.

When I started upstream it was tough but after while it wasn't as tough as in the beginning. After walking in the water for awhile the time passed quickly and the water started to get a little higher and stronger, but I kept pushing on. The thought of going downstream still seemed easier, and then the still voice assured me that I would be alright, but I was so tired. Out of the corner of my eye I saw a big flat rock resembling a platform. I climbed up on it and rested for awhile. And then the voice said, "In me you'll find rest". Once again I was revived but I just sat there watching everyone going by and having a good time. Now that the hour was getting late the number of people increased. Some of the same people that were going upstream were now drifting downstream. But the gentle nudging was still there as I continued upstream. It was dark and the water continued to rise and had cooled off which made it uncomfortable. But now I had a determination that wouldn't let me stop, yes it was dark, but I could still see. I slowed my pace but still kept going. As day break came there seemed to be even more people going downstream. They invited me to come along but there was uncertainty in their voices. I saw some of my old buddies and hung out with them for awhile. When I started back upstream I felt as if I had wasted a lot of time. And sure enough some things that I had already seen were passing me by again. That's when I realized that even though it felt like I was standing still, I had drifted downstream. The time that I had lost was very precious. Now the water had all sorts of material things floating down and I needed to make up for all of the time I had lost. This created many obstacles; it wasn't a straight path anymore. I saw my uncle and now that I felt more confident I tried to encourage him to come with me, but he just waved and continued down the river. The inner voice told me that there was an end to the river that no would be able to survive. I traveled this path for many days, months and years. I've seem many things going downstream. I even stopped off a few more times myself. Upon returning to my journey upstream I witnessed a few who were now fighting against the current. When we reached the top the first thing I noticed was the things that use to be important to me weren't important anymore. I felt complete; the weight of the water that had absorbed in my clothing had washed away. The water was so still that it resembled a large mirror. The grass was greener than any grass I had ever seen before. I had the urge to look back, but the still voice said "don't look back". As I continued on my journey it only got better. There were family and familiar people there waiting for me. They took me to my mansion and everything I had lost along the way was there, and so much more.

Linda Hart –Washington

<u>Mamma and Daddy's Room</u>

In mamma bedroom we were never allowed to go
But I wanted to watch TV and my brothers were
playing Nintendo
I was at the foot of the bed being quite and the TV
was real low
All the lights were out except the TV glow
When Momma and Daddy came in I slid under
the footboard bench
Trying to figure how I was gonna get out when…
Daddy said come on women and the bed sunk in
I started to crawl like a marine in basic training
under a wire fence
I was sweatin and my heart was beating when I
heard mamma say
Stop Scott I hear something… I froze then she
moaned and he grunted
 I knew they was naked but I couldn't see nothing
I got out of there but I couldn't close the door so I
left it cracked
When I became grown I heard the same grunt in
my room
That same moan in my own tone and just like
 Mamma and Daddy's room We wasn't alone.
GO TO BED SON!!!!

KB

Say Something™

3 FLESH

Uprooted

As I am spiritually awakened by a tearing of my own flesh the pain is much too great for any physical form of words,

As I hit the ground I stretch out and offer a loud and deep grown from within that only those of the spiritual realm could understand,

Everything that I've grown accustomed to is now being torn away from me. My separation causes yet another discomfort,

My exposed roots whisper truths that cause judgments,

Everything about me has been covered with rich dark soil nurtured by the laws of the earth,

Everything that I've suffered was wrapped in the dark earth protected by silence, never to be told,

The water trembles as my long lasting roots are snatched from its shelter,

Extensions of me that have been entangled are now being pulled away,

I lay still as the sun dries out the ends of my future, the crackling of my flesh sounds in my own ears,

I cry out but there's no answer, my beautiful roots are now brown because I am hungry and need nourishment,

Grown Folks

Rest leaves me because of this sudden change, I am
vulnerable and the beasts now threaten my very soul,

I lay weak and worried about my destination

Your promises seem so far away, my pulse is faint and death
hovers over me,

The winds whisper things of my exposed roots and the
whispers carry far and wide,
Just when I thought all of my worries were over and I had
adjusted for the end,

You sent the winds back, strong and powerful blowing in
every direction, even those who judged me were now being
uprooted,

You blew me in the cool waters that were now in
disagreement with you, the heat and dryness lifted from my
now singed roots and comfort wrapped itself around me once
again,

The healing process was great through your ministry, you
said that you would never leave nor forsake me, the life in the
water removed that which was dried and withered and you
restored me,

Now my roots have taken to new soil, shooting in every
direction, driving deep down below the rivers bed to discover
new life,

You have uprooted and replanted me and now again I live.
Linda Hart - Washington

Flesh Is Weak

Trying to escape my flesh and live in my
spiritual being
The flesh I see and the flesh is hungry
Reluctantly, I feed
However, good eats
At time it's just gluttonous indulging in
abundance
I call on my spirit man to recue me from
this beast
He doesn't always come when I call but
just in the nick of time
Never feeling I have won
Hard knowing
The growls and rumbles will again come
I live in the spirit man at peace
Until it's time to feed.

Grown Folks

I DID'NT HEAR YOU CALLING

*I DID'NT HEAR YOU CALLING, SO I LET MYSELF BE
LED ASTRAY,
TOO EAGER WAS A WEAKENED HEART TO HEAR SWEET
NOTHING FROM ANOTHER.
BY TOMORROW I MAY BE SOMEWHAT CONSCIOUS TO MY
MISGIVINGS OR YOUR FORGIVINGS..*

BUT TODAY, TONIGHT,

*FORGIVE ME NOT BECAUSE I HAVE WILLINGLY
SUCCUMBED TO ALL MENTAL STROKES AND PHYSICAL
PROMISES.
I DID'NT HEAR YOU CALLING AND DUE TO THIS
SMALL TECHNICALITY,
I TURNED MY BACK AND SANG FOR THE NIGHT WAS
YOUNG AND THE SPIRIT WAS SO QUITE ABLE,
AND OH SO WILLING.*

*I DANCED A WICKED WALTZ TO TWILIGHTS
MESMORIZING LYRICS,
BLANKETS OF DARKNESS,
CRICKETS AND SUCH.
THEY LA LA LA'D RIGHT INTO MY HEART,
THEY SEDUCED ME,
AND I FROLICKED WITHIN THE PONDS OF ANXIOUS,
EXHILITERATING EXPECTATIONS OVER AND OVER.
LONI ROSS*

Grown Folks

I WAS ME TONIGHT,
NO NOT THE BUSINESS SUIT, TIGHT BUNNED,
HORNED RIMMED, CALCULATOR CLICKING ME.
BUT FINALLY THE LETTING GO,
RUNNING BAREFOOT THROUGH THE GRASS,
EXPERIENCING TOUCH, FEARLESS FOR THE SAKE OF
LIVIMG IN THIS EXQUISITE MOMENT ME,
AND THE SENSUALITY OF THE MOMENT WAS
BREATHTAKING.

MY SENSES WERE OVERPOWERED WITH THE AROMA OF
A NEW FOUND PLEASURE,
IT WAS TRUELY INTOXICATING.
AND THE TOUCH SET OFF A THOUSAND MATCHES IN
MY BODY,
IGNITING FLESH THAT I WAS TOLD WAS THE ENEMY.
IF THIS BE TRUE,
THEN THE ENEMY ENTERTAINED WITH ME THIS
EVENING AND BED ME AS IF IT ALWAYS
WAITED PATIENTLY IN THE SHADOWS,
KNOWING I WOULD GIVE IN ONE DAY.

AND I DID, WHY, BECAUSE THEY CALLED OUT SO
LOUD FOR ME THIS DAY,
THAT I COULD NO LONGER HEAR, YOUR WHISPERS
REGARDING MY
INADEQUACIES.

LONI ROSS

Co-Co Butta……. By SD Howard

Co-Co Butta……. that's the color of your skin and I been watching and I'm thinking that the extent of yo sin, I'm gon win with this devilish ass grin.... Looking at you across the room and knowin that there's gonna be some doom when you make that ass go boom all over me.... This is the place to be and what I imagine Isoo want you to see.... So come real close and enjoy the ride, I won't hide what's inside cause just the thought of it keeps me alive……

I looked at you when you got out the tub as I wanted to mall you, but I set my needs aside... There you are standing there all thick and ready and I'm listening to my insides as they start to breathing real heavy.... Man meat getting real thick and got some things that he want to get in and seek but you know you're so unique and I'm gonna make sure this ain't just a peek..... coming over real slow and taking your hand and walking you over to the bed as you so in the hell modeling that red... damn a nicca only thinking about being fed but I can't take it there I know you ain't got on NO underwear and it perplexing me and vexing me but that's gonna be a part of the next episode you see.... Yeah baby that's all me that you reached down and touched don't want it to start a fuss cause if you must you can take him out and marvel at him cause I know that you got some plans to do, what you do. I see you licking them lips as you dip those hip deep off onto that bed..... looking at them fantastic ass thighs and just knowing that I just wanna do real bad things to you.

Neva

Taking the string to that rob in my mouth and pulling it down south as you lay back with a gentle shove, I'm about to open up your area and show you this love, first hand.. Taking your legs in my hand and pushing them up to the heavens and listening to you as take in those deep breaths as I get comfortable... I'm molding you to the bed so you can get this fiya ass head.... Now you ain't dead but this mission in me was born and bred....As I take my time and lick you from side to side I know that you ain't really ready for this ride but there ain't nothing left for me to hide... I've told you from time to time that this is what I do but today if all about what a nicca can show you... Do you approve of the way I move cause I fuccin up yo insides to the groove of that slow jam that you got playing in the back ground.... Yeah I love the sounds that you keep making as those thighs are shaking and you really had me mistaken... for that one that needed to take a break and get some rest...

Neva a test, I don't claim to be the best but when I'm done, you'll sing a song cause of that mental and physical rum that I just laid on you..... Kitty is speaking back to me right now in tongue.... Oooooo damn, what fun, this is.... As my face is drenched in the juices that have flown from within you.. I slide my way up your body slowly, allowing each and every inch of him to touch the inner parts of your thigh as my tongue has now made his way to those already aroused nips that were patiently waiting their turn.... Slowly and gently taking them in my mouth one at a time as you grab me down there cause you clit can't take not another bump from that big ass lump that has crawled right up against her.. I can feel your fingers wrapping around me tightly as you guide him to the spot where you need taking care of the most..... I don't mean to boast but this feeling that I'm having is the most... amazing thing that I've ever been a part of... Damn..the water starts to flow as soon as I breech the walls... I love it cause the moisture pulls me in even closer... damn..... as I feel you grab my ass and push me deeper....

Looking deep into your eyes as I grip your thighs as you bit your lips and I dip yo hips.... I don't want it to end but I can feel that kitty biting back and I'm just trying to give it right back as I dig my knees in the bed and give you all of the big phat head.... real deep and slow and you tell me you want more..... now it's a lil faster pace cause now I can see that look on your face as you take that pillow and put it in place.... where about to have lift off and I just want that magic send off, now the speed has gotten a lil ferocious and we getting it in like two beast on point.... this here is my joint.... One last good thrust and you buss then I buss.... and the way you grab my head was truly a must........ Yeah, this is why you got that name and I don't have anyone to blame..........

Co-Co Butter...... and that's all that cream I got in my lap right now......... Dammmmmmmn

Grown Folks

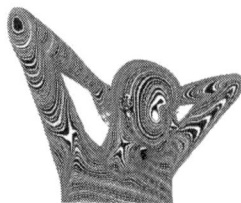

Sex is Overrated

You tell everyone "I don't care", well I'm
here to call your bluff
cause every cute guy you meet, you
eventually give a fuck
and only when he peaks feelings released
resemble love
and after about a week you notice he 's
giving up
It takes you about a season to officially give
him up.
He don't judge a book by its cover, he tends
to peek at the back
and when he felt he was being smothered
he left and never looked back
I warned you about that type baby girl
matter of fact
I showed you a perfect example of exactly
how to act
and you acting like you're naive cause your
heart is not intact
and this man you let deceive hoping that he
can place it back
but he didn't, now its missing, let me kiss it
… just like that

Grown Folks

I feel it, I won't conceal it, I know you
feeling it too
I'd rather we not have sex girl I just met you
I want your heart not your parts, let this
kiss be a start
Pray that I mend it to begin with and we
don't drift apart
because sex is overrated, used as
manipulation
abused as imitation to gain what is sacred
thinking that you found love
then your heart gets misplaced in
a sticky situation your heart remains vacant
steady searching for love
in all the wrong places
oh baby baby don't give into the lust

- Aaron Smith aka Poetic NJustice

with ringlets of your body hair decorating each
one,
Bringing to the surface of my skin the passion of
unspoken words,
acted out by your warm mouth on my body,
Your fingertips leaving lasting trails of
impressions
familiar with each curve of my body,
creating a pool in my most private places,
Mastering my flesh with locked eyes,
hands and mouth,
Each part of me waiting patiently for your arrival,
Filling empty spaces, dry places,
smiles on faces, entering welcomed places,
Hunger pains claim a constant yearning for you,
your touch, your smile…

Linda Hart - Washington

Passion Filled ...... SD Howard

Woke up real thick and ready for something real good to eat, there you were still laying there underneath the sheets... yeah I can still taste that flavor that's so unique... It makes me weak to know that every time I touch you I can't help but reach my peek.... taking my time as I reach for the cover and slowly pull them off you. I don't want to disturb you cause this treat I have in store is sure gonna curb, your appetite. I know that the passion that's running thru me can't be matched so I can't wait to look in the mirror and see that arch in yo back.... damn my hunger has come right back, that shit is wack, but this time imma take a crack, at making you feel so amazing that you understand that this sex is blazin............

Moving the covers off as I take my hands and run them up your thigh, just to say hi to your imagination... Makin passes between those thighs and to my surprise they open wide with nothing to hide cause all along you were ready for this ride.... Looking up into those eyes and I see you with that sneaky smile, yeah you been waiting for quite a while but you ain't mild, but you really do have a wild side...... so don't hide I'll oblige and give you all that you want inside.......

Tongue gently stroking those mysterious places.... understanding that there is no need for racing I have a wonderful view from where my face is.... yeah I like it like that and this right here is gonna get me a plaque cause I'm a master and it's gonna be a disaster once

I'm done you might have enough to plaster... that feeling all over your face yeah cause I'm gonna take care of every need underneath yo waist..... Hands take control of those thighs as I search deep inside, don't hide...... let yo nature rise... sucking real gentle trying reach inside yo mental make a peaceful explosion full of emotions.... yeah like that..... Arch that back and give this head game a crack...

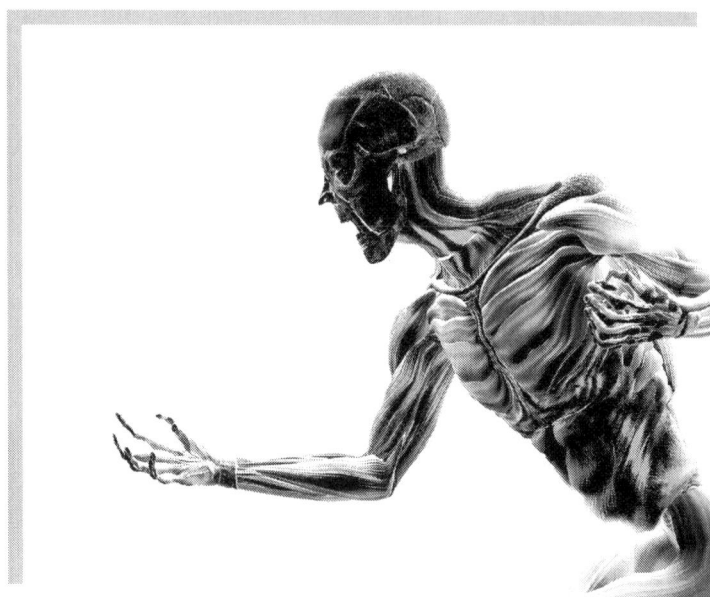

The Skin I'm In

See me,
Feel me,
Breath me,
Allow me to be yours,
Allow me to be touched,
Allow me to open wide,
Sweet berries inside,
Stir, stir,
Until we make the sweetest of blends,
Defend my thighs,
And I will permit you to rise,
The honey in the hive with a nectar equal to or
greater.
Lips thick with yes...yes...yes,
Moans within the ears of "Baby you're the best",
Twist and turns,
Releasing yearns,
Greed and lust...permittence of frequent rope
burns
Last push and pants,
Spoon one way, now turn,
See me,
Feel me,
Breath me,
Love this skin I'm in

LONI ROSS

Flesh

The desire to acquire a fire that never tires
sensation temptation complacent with
trading places
indecent exposure mixed with thoughts
beyond sober
pulsating veins pulses rapidly sustain
while repeating ones name
privates part then reenter silent stalks then
screams center
wet as snowflakes and rain drops
peaks resembling a roar from the depths of
mountain tops
no cameras but eventually Imax and
relations get shipped like I faxed
climax hot as burning wax as I dial tones
after searching through my contacts
I contact to make eye contact then eyes role
beyond that
no hesitation straight to the head her name
is miss education

the basics in bed overshadowed by the
matrix
numbers never lie but while we're lying
she's complacent
confidence is obvious through sensation
and conversation
i would say she's acceptable the way she's
taking it
we climax at the same time, empathy's next
slippery wet energies mesh through our
sensitive flesh

- Aaron Smith aka Poetic NJustice

If Loving You...

I keep hearing the song, "if loving you is wrong,

Upside down, right-side up, up to no good, good
God, good grief, good ass lovin even as I sleep,

Sleepin in to get another piece, peace creeps
within and righteousness' grabs hold to
consciousness and here I go again singing the
song, if loving you is wrong,

As I rise I strive to throw off the covers, covering
myself, my head my lover and the bed,

I head home trying to forget all that I remember
about what I don't know, and where I won't go,
but have gone,

I'm wrong for being right, now begins the fight, I
battle with myself about selfishness and shame,
the same shame I lost too last week as the
memories creep in my head, reminding me that I
said, never again, but again I say 'if loving you is
wrong' yeah!

So I'm not right because imma keep loving you, I
keep repeating what I won't do, as Paul said,
'those things I don't want to do, I do,

I'm not in love, but I keep on loving you, I can't see you anymore, but I find myself leaving you, if loving you is wrong…

I'm bruised now after beating myself up, but I was promised to drink from the fathers cup, the cup overturned and the promises spilled, and as I shower hell creeps inside me again,

I know loving you is wrong, but the next line I won't say, I use it as a drug to keep me away, cause the habit of an addict is usually this way,

So imma go ahead and take a nap, take a shot and then I'll be back, cause I don't want to do right…

Linda Hart - Washington

Grown Folks

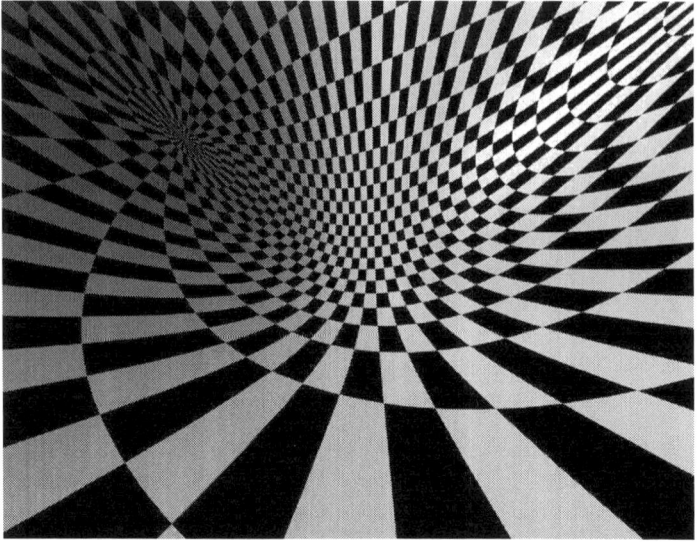

Thought They Had Me... PT 1   by SD Howard

Yeah todays the day and I'm going all out. She called me and gave me the directions and told me to just bring my imagination and something strong to drink cause what she had planned for me was gonna be an all-nighter.. So you know me and from the start this was a challenge so you know I'm game for anything. I made sure to get fresh and put that smell good in all the right places cause I don't want for her to be making them sad faces....

Here I am at the door and all I can think is that this night is about to jump off and I just want it to be all that I dreamed it out to be... Yeah you been talking ish to me for days but that I'm not gonna hold against you but I will put something in you to let you know that I'm not a play toy but I can help you with a few games that you might wanna play. Knock knock and there you are standing there in the door with that sexy ass outfit that has my mouth on the floor... and all I can think about is doing bad things to you in more ways than one. Not even saying a word to me as you just turn and walk away and here I am following like a lil puppy because you got all the treats that I'm looking for. I know that you want me as much as I want you but today is the day that I want you to know that I'm not like anyone else. Walking up to you real fast and pushing you on the bed and looking you deep in those sexy ass eyes as you know what's about to go down.

Taking my place between those thighs as I wrap them up on my forearms as I spread them a lil wider so that you pucci can meet this friend that I brought along with me, as I slowly lick my way down your inner thigh and listen to the moans that are coming outta your mouth and that smile come out like no other because I'm in my area now. I can hear the music playing in the background but never once did it make me think to stop as I took no time to introduce my tongue to your insides..... sucking on your clit ever so slowly as I flickered around her and sucked on each and every piece of you. Just as I was getting into it like no other I felt a second set of hands caressing my body and it felt so damn good...... Taking a look over you into the mirror on the head board and I could see her up against my back in that sexy red teddy, that brown skin pressed up against me an those nipples extra hard up against my back but this is what I wanted......

Yeah my dicc is supa thick now as I am about to loose control but Nicca here has got to be on a role...... yeah you brought me here but I have so gotta finish this mission.... grabbin your real tight and pullin that kitty even closer to my face as I feel her take my manhood into her hands awwwwwwwwwwhhh dammmmmmmn this wasn't supposed to happen like this.....

To Be Continued........

Grown Folks

Thought They Had Me..... PT 2   by SD Howard

Yeah my dicc is supa thick now as I am about to loose control but Nicca here has got to be on a role...... yeah you brought me here but I have so gotta finish this mission.... grabbin your real tight and pullin that kitty even closer to my face as I feel her take my manhood into her hands awwwwwwwwwwhhh dammmmmmmn this wasn't supposed to happen like this....

Just as she grabbed me it made me suck just a lil harder... sorry baby but dammmmmnn that shit feels good.. as you laid there and she slide down to her knees and took me inside her mouth all I could think was, Dammmmm I can't let this thing.. so I reached over and grabbed the bottle of wine you had on the side and I took a swig as I felt those lips wrap around me like no other... She sucked on me as I sucked on you and what a lovely noise we where making...... just then I took a finger and began rubbing it against your clit and I quickly felt you wrap your legs around my waist as to not explode all over the place. That lil hit has got me for a minute plus it took my mind off it and put me back where I needed to be... slowly sliding my fingers inside trying not to hide the fact that this has been a dream of mine while she's taking her time pleasing me.... Dammmmmmmn..

My dicc is thick and almost ready to spit so I have to pick her up too and taste some of her clit... pushing her up on top of you on all fours and watching you two kiss has me going a lil crazy in my mind, but

54

dammmmmmmn that shiiiit is real sexy to me... as I know have two pretty kitties staring back at me.... as I take her azz cheeks and spread them wide to see what types of treasures are deep off inside. Watching her suck your breast as you prepare to take in the rest..... Slowly taking my hand and guiding my man inside those dripping wett walls of yours..... yeah just like that as you try your best to keep in that sound but I can tell that it gonna be heard round town... first silent then a whimper and then an all-out moan... this is the shit that I can't leave alone.

Diggin deep off in you and slappin her ass like she stole something from me.... I feel those juices floating around all over me as I take a few short jabs then push all up in you and hearing those sounds that I long for... Next I take him out and let her take a taste as I prepare to give her all she can handle from the back.... giving that azz a good smack.... yeah baby I'm back and I don't plan on letting this one die down cause never will I be thought of as a clown..... Yeah she tries her best to take control by pushin that kitty all up against this dicc but in an instant it takes control.... yeah and all she has is you to hold as those juices start to explode in and around her..... Yeah this is what I do when I do........

Naw this is just the beginning and we ain't done yet........

Secrets...

Mmmmmm, my secrets I hold deep inside,
I'm a good girl with a conniving side,
because I want what I want and I ain't
afraid to wait you out,
and you will be mine, it's just a matter of
time,
this I have no doubt.
To some I'm a nerd that happens to be easy
on the eyes,
they don't know that this chick does flips
when shown the vulnerable side,
hips spread wide, eager for you to come
inside,
I'll hold you all night til the walls crumble
inside.
A sucker for true emotions,
talks of passion, devotion...
talks of fears....trail of tears,
suddenly I can't keep my hands off you
and at my side.
Never knew it could be like this,
a simple kiss and I become vulnerable to
your special blend of bliss,
so I try to keep from looking you in the

eyes,
I stay far from your touch,
I even play it neutral on the phone...
you don't need to know, that 3rd glass of
wine,
Is my kryptonite,
and if you ask me right,
I may take you home with me tonight,
Cause secretly I love climbing the walls
from a 3am booty call,
It's always been my weakness,
giving into my sexual secrets.
Shhhhhhh......don't tell, just come over for a
spell,
I can cook, we can talk or we
can.........mmmmmmmm

LONI ROSS

Say Something™

4 LOVE

I Once Was A Child

Who will protect the children?
When we stand and fight over whose wrong and
right
While they stand, cry lay in wait
While the judge (courts) determine their fate

Who will protect the children?
When we drop them off at the church house door
From the well disguised child molester
While we praising the Lord on the second floor

Who will protect the children?
When we leave for work
From the daycare provided
Whipping on them and feeding them dirt

Who will protect the children?
When we send them to school
From the beast released with gun and no rules
While we stand, cry and lay in wait
While the judge (God) determines our fate
KB

She Oak Tree

As I look upon her, she reminds me of the oak tree
in the back...yard
Back of my head... my mind wonders off to a
place where she stood firm by the waters
Firmly standing... standing up against the
unwanted winds, storms, stones...
Stones thrown from across the waters of time to
intimidate the thick bark that covered her and
never penetrating her protective cover, thick skin,
dark skin, strong skin, beautiful black skin...
Skin of her teeth, teeth torn out by the roots from
malnutrition and anger from gritting through the
night, instead of a good night's sleep...
Sleep to escape the chopping down of pride and
love...
Loving one's self, one another and others, lending
herself to scribble their thoughts upon, a dilution
of her strength...
Strength to hold on, to hold on to, mother earth,
produced me, who is a mother too...
To grow and produce, to cover... cover me and
you with shelter, from my limb, to make lumber,
for cottages and mansions...
Mansions given to some, but promised to all...
All who know their roots, who know the truth,
who sits a spell under the oak tree, under she,
under me,
Piling the rocks thrown to pave a way or start a
rock quarry to use another day...

Day in and day out, expecting when there's a
drought…
Drought from knowledge and hope, putting your
trust in green leaves to smoke…
Smoke goes up and disappear, into thin air this
atmosphere,
Minds wonder and dreams are born, only to be
stolen and soon gone,
Break a cycle, break the chains, that bare the last
name, to receive, to claim, like a dismembered tree
forced to shame,
Name a baby, name a dog, brand a tree, to claim a
log, for ownership and personal use, personal
abuse, need no excuse and free to reduce ones
pride and royalty…
Under the oak tree, under she, under me~

Linda Hart – Washington

Grown Folks

Domestic Violence

Let me take the wheel just relax while I steer
I'll stare into your eyes as I swim in the depth of your
tears
and if you on the edge then I'll remain the peer
I usually only feel at my peak when you near
if complexion hasn't taught a thing just know we in a
race
all your steps retake as I determine the pace
I'll control your breath and predetermine your fate
your heart is so fragile but please don't break
you keep juggling with it but let me hold it wait
like a vault's combination it may be safe
depending on how you guard it, but just wait
while you try and harness I will reach it regardless
when ladies don't acknowledge this I grow lethargic
your guard up like Love don't penetrate targets
from the back or missionary it just varies how she
wants it
Some say that I'm blunt like there's one in my pocket
but in all actuality I'm just being honest
back to this woman whose beauty should be
acknowledged
my heart you can land on, forget sharecropping
your ex man beat you down up was not an option
I'm here to uplift because what's beauty without
confidence?
A painstaking consciousness with very little tolerance

no incentive to complement and beatings help you
condescend
How can you think you in Love when you in and out
of consciousness?
Love is not having to lie just to protect your kids
Love is not fear, Love is not tears
Love is not bruises after a couple beers
with a whole lot of anger and a little bit of cheers
Love is fear that he'll leave, not that he's on the way
Love is tears that he's left, not that he won't go away
Love is lying on the bed together knowing that you'll
be okay
Love is scars healing on your heart from yesterday's
pain
Love is what I present Love is the fact that I am present
Love is not a black eye and sunglasses as a present
Love shouldn't be covered up love is something
excellent
Love should be broadcasted not violence that's
domestic

-    Aaron Smith aka Poetic NJustice

I Work Hard... ... ...SD Howard

There you are with that look in your eyes while I sit here and look at all those pics that I've seen so many times. My mind runs wild each and every time I think of the things that I want to do to you. I have thought of the time that I would have with you in my arms and you just being able to allow me to do the things that I have envisioned all along.

That bath water was run for you and I was sitting here waiting on you so that I can show you how much I appreciate all that you do. I never want you to think that I don't see the things that you do for me as I take your hand as you walk thru that door... Yeah, I want this to be the greatest day ever. Watching you as your outstretched leg reaches up over the side of the tub as you take one foot after the other and take a seat. I've waited so long to be able to put my hands on you in such a way... Taking that towel and lathering it up as you lay your head back and smell the aroma of the bath beads and the incents that I have all around you.
Taking that hand and slowly running it along your side and taking your foot with the other hand as I lift it out of the water and place it on my chest as I wash it ever so slowly, making sure not to miss a spot... softly as I slowly lower that one down and repeat with the other... Laughing at the way that you are looking at me... "What," is what I say and I already know what you're thinking....

I'm looking real deep into those beautiful eyes as you look right back as my hand has gotten comfortable and is beginning to roam freely into those wonderful spaces that have caused quite an erection in my lower regions... I'm leaning in to accept those sexy ass lips of yours as you take your hand and wrap your fingers around the back of my neck as you pull me closer. Never once did I hear any negative thoughts so I proceeded to make happy faces right along with you... Feeling those lips as my fingers ventured between the other set as my free hand took control of those gorgeous breast of yours...... I can't help but think that this is all and some compared to what I was wanting and I'm gonna make sure that you know that this is where I wanted to be anyway. The water play has us both feeling a little giddy as you whisper in my ear, "Baby don't be too gentle" and with that I know that the time has come...... ...

Creeping Desires
Silken words like hands creeping up my thigh
causing the heat to simmer,
the lips to part,
causing one's breath to sigh.
Delicious streams of moonlit rays dance across my
round, swollen breast,
I arch at their request,
for only you know my true weakness,
my strengths,
how to awaken my passion,
and how to put this fire to rest.
I sit in the center of my bed,
chin on my bent knees,
watching you want me.
My soul sits naked before you,
my inhibitions anticipate you,
my most secret thoughts on display for you.,
my soft, wet, bronze like flesh waiting to be kissed
by the bleeding portrait that only your beautiful
strokes can provide.
Your eyes devour me before your physical aura
ever takes flight,
but once in motion,
your lips,
your tongue,
your hands,
your mighty thrust open the night and
I become yours as you become mine.
I tremble and shudder for I have become your
tongues prisoner

and I watch as you elude such power
as you invade between my legs over and over,
causing me to cry rivers,
causing me to scream from the mountains
causing me to bow before you and beg.
In the dead of the night as I sleep alone,
I hear you step from your throne,
I feel you come for me.
Nowhere for me to hide as you creep into my
moans,
so I lay back ,
open wide
and give your desires a happy home.

LONI ROSS

He is...

With his eyebrows raised and arms crossed, he seeks out the infinite possibilities of his future,

Intellectually down to earth and intelligently abound, there is no limit to his highs even when the lows present themselves,

Determined to apply himself completely, while patiently waiting, for not just the fruit of his labor, but the juice from the fruit to be poured out and distributed, as diluting the fruit causes his blessings to go even further,

no not one selfish bone exists in his body, but giving, giving of all that he is, he has, because he understands that in giving the reward is much greater,

He is blessed and because of that blessing his seed is blessed, a teacher with the ability to enrich any level of being, high or low, rich or poor

He places high expectations of himself in exceeding and conquering the known and unknown to his own understanding,

Loving completely all that he has taken unto himself, and loving more that which was given him, increasing and fine tuning the man he has come to know, to be presented,

Who seeks out the infinite possibilities of his future,

He is...

Linda Hart –Washington

It Had to Happen... ... by SD Howard

Never in my mind was there a thought that I couldn't control this situation.. The lust that I saw in your eyes was of complete and utter devastation. With me being the person that I am, I couldn't think of another place that I would rather be. You touch me in so many ways and each and every time I've allowed you to elude me. This times I need that gentle touch to soothe me... I want you to caress me while those hands and lips undress me. What a tangled inner space we're in but never the less this is that place where we both will win.

Your voice had a way of intoxicating me and put me in places that I really didn't want to be but I accepted it, and relished it because I knew that without you there was NO other mix that I wanted. Diving deep into your arms and placing my tongue deep off in your ear.... Yeah that's what I do when your near... with no fear all I wanna do is release your inner cheer... Yeah the excitement I won't deny it but with the personal emotions the richest man couldn't buy it...

I really don't know what to do about the way I feel about you cause every single time I constantly think of what you mean to me... I can't seem to shake you but I know what I can't have really might not break me....I'm rambling with all of these emotions but I know in the back of my mind that you got that supa love potion..... give it to me and give it to me well, I promise from now on there won't be a story that I won't tell .... about you.

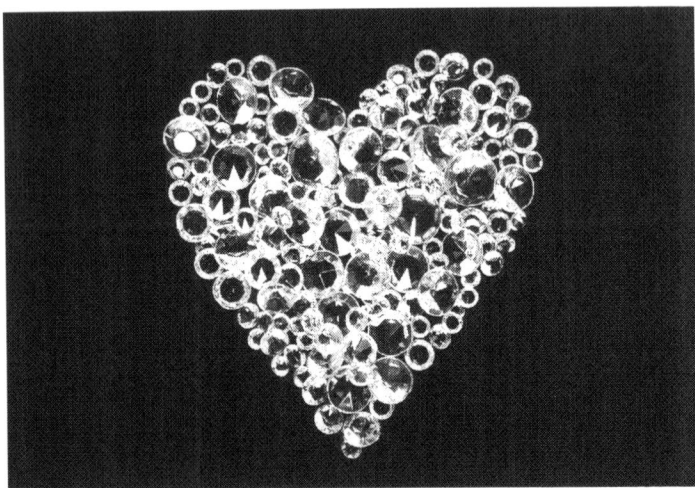

I think my brush has a crush on him,
So simple, so crisp,
So cool to the touch,
He's the perfect specimen I want to touch with my
virgin brush,
I think my brush has a crush on him.

Oh to be a color in his world,
Shades of majesty,
That eloquent shimmer upon his pearls,
Splattered melodies that excite the eyes,
I think my brush has a crush on him.

My brush wants to sing you a song,
Sweeter than the humming bird hums,
More vibrant than the calypso's steel drum,
More stirring than the strums from a Spanish
Guitar,
Mi cepillo le adora y todos los colores de
magníficas que eres
I think my brush has a crush on him.

My brush daydreams of frequent sips on your
potent fragrance,
You have it giddy with your come hither scent,
Like the bee to honey,
Your abundant spaciousness keep me coming,
You let me in and I am forever in your debt.

My ink is stale whenever we are apart,
Fluid and life giving when you are close by my

Grown Folks

heart,
Blessings are given,
In your direction I'm driven,
Your Beauteous physic has mesmerized mine
fingers from the very start.

My brush has a crush on him,
His strength is beyond compare,
He has become the moon and the stars to me,
I call him Mural for he has become larger than life,
I celebrate your allure and my captivity...
For you have become the exquisite 16th Chapel to
my modern day Michelangelo
My brush has a crush on him...

LONI ROSS

Love, Peace and Serenity

Love peace and serenity never hate your enemy
if you stand for nothing you will fall for anything
if you're in my vicinity than you are now a friend
to me
even if you're far away just twitter mention me
your soul lasts until infinity
while your body is a temporary home rented by
your entity
hate fuels a cold world love is warm like humidity
daunting tasks can be quenched providing energy
as long as there are oceans close in the vicinity
my passion will increase as my pen leaks with
more intensity
the whole earth is my home so homelessness can
never enter me
my body is my temple and my soul shares its
empathy
they say love is hard to find but to me it's getting
clearer
you can never find true Love until you find it in
the mirror
cause in reality that guy cupid could never help
Love is only hard to find if you don't look within
yourself

- Aaron Smith aka Poetic NJustice

5 ENLIGHTMENT

Grown Folks

Bridging The Gaps
In American education there are many many gaps
with increasingly diverse schools all across the map
despite the many tools used
the playing field is hard to level
because while some students remain homeless
others couldn't be living better
some students struggle just to listen
to what the teacher repetitively mentions
and other students are autistic
or just always in detention
with lower levels of retention
some are Muslim; others Christian
while some never even heard of the word religion
so as teachers we must take into account all diversities
whether culturally, psychologically, or physically
whatever they may be
As we construct to build the future and extend
pathways overseas
we must bridge the gaps in between so we can prepare
all to succeed
and as we pave the way by example is how we must
lead

-   Aaron Smith aka Poetic NJustice

<u>Army of God Will Rein In</u>

I aint scared of you devil
I am better
I won't give you power
Believing ever bad thing you rein
Bible 1 Corinthians 11
 God is over and above all. Everything comes from
God,
Knowing now that not everything is good but
You aint Michael Jackson BAD
You're limited in speech
You only whisper to the weak
We only hear when in a state of disbelieve
I know what you know
How you were conceived from fire
Me made from clay and
You were still made to bow before me
Your anger is your rage
Knowing our God's love for man is great
Man is strong alone, Greater in numbers
On the Day of Judgment we will remember
Surah 3:54 Yusuf Ali
And the disbelievers planned, but Allah planned. And
Allah is the best of planners
You whispered in our hearts
Tried to convince us we're not worthy to live
To destroy the earth, kill each other and our kids
I no longer live in fear
The army of God is here
Let us rein and put the devil to shame.
KB

My Inner Waterfall

Thank you God, for you are my inner waterfall.
I am constantly being shaped and formed to the
perfection you created me to be.
In your eyes I am perfect, because you made me in
your image;
You cover me and hide me with your cool water,
I never thirst because your waters are forever
flowing,
For who can be thirsty when they are in you,
Your waters run over me, cleansing me. Washing
away all that is not meant to be a part of me,
Those things that have drifted downstream and
settled among me,
Because of your continual care, they can not
remain,
Even things that I've stopped from flowing down
stream because of my own selfishness, Because of
your patience you allowed me to hold on to
broken branches and debris until I was ready to let
go, and by letting go I've grown,
I've filled yet another empty space because of you,
The broken glass that was trapped between the
rocks has washed away,
Because you slowed down the waters to relieve
the pressure that kept it there,
But even it was there as long as it needed to be,
It caused much pain, but its reflection was
beautiful to look upon,

Grown Folks

My rough edges have become smooth. Rot and
decay have been washed away,
I know that no one could have done that for me
but you,
You've not left me and your cool blanket still
covers me,
My tears can no longer be seen because they have
become a part of your constant flowing waters,
You have separated me from all others, but I'm
never alone. As long as I have you I'm complete,
Everything that I need is provided for me, I just
have to understand my own need, Sometimes
visitors come and climb all over me. I thank you
for providing sturdy ground for them,
Leaving behind old debris and taking up new.
Please make them aware of your presence,
sometimes death and stench wash downstream,
but the life in the water revive me and cause it to
pass by,
After a storm I get backed up and swell feeling as
if I'm drowning, you create an out and the dam is
broken and all flows free again,
While the waters we're swollen and high and I felt
unsafe you still showed me the beauty in it,
When I need to learn a lesson you rise above me in
a mist, but you're still there,
When I call to you, you make your presence
known to me,
Even when I'm rustling your rushing waters never
end,

When visitors see us they are overtaken by the
beauty you've placed upon me.
It's the inner waterfall that keeps me as white as
snow, as bright as noonday and as fresh as spring,
You never stop perfecting me and for that I thank
you.

Linda Hart – Washington

EACH DAY I AWAKE TO YOUR TOUCH,
YOUR WARMTH FLOODS ME,
YOUR SMILE CAPTIVATES ME,
YOUR EVERESCENT GLOW ILLUMINATES,
YOU AWAKEN MY SOUL AND WITH THE
ARCHING OF MY BODY I RECEIVE YOU AND
ALL YOUR SPLENDOR.
NEVER ONCE HAVE I DOUBTED THE
SINCERITY OF YOUR TOUCH,
OR THAT YOU WOULD ALWAYS BE THERE
FOR ME,
FROM THE FIRST DAY THAT WE MET,
YOU HAVE BEEN MY ONE AND ONLY.
YOU ENFOLD ME SO LOVINGLY THAT TEARS
ARE FOREVER FLOWING DOWN MY FACE
WHEN I THINK OF YOU.
YOUR AURA INVADES MY BODY ON A DAILY
BASIS AND IT'S LIKE THE RIPPLES ON THE
OCEAN
THAT EVENTUALLY BECAME A TITLE WAVE
AND I CAN SUPPRESS MY EMOTIONS FOR
YOU NO
LONGER.
YOU INTOXICATE ME WITH YOUR WORDS,
I FOLLOW YOU ABOUT LIKE THE CHILDREN
TO THE PIED PIPER'S FLUTE,
YOUR STRENGTH HAS BECOME THE ARMOR
THAT ENCIRCLES MY LIFE,
MY DEVOTION TO YOU IS UNWAVERING
AND I BOW BEFORE YOU WITHOUT SHAME.
WE TURN HEADS WHEREVER WE GO

BECAUSE
YOU HOLD ME,
YOU TEACH ME,
YOU NEVER LET ME STRAY,
YOU PROTECT ME,
YOU LOVE ME.
AND I HAVE BECOME YOUR HUMBLE,
OBEDIENT STUDENT ALWAYS,
AND AS I CLOSE MY EYES BESIDE YOU,
YOU COVET ME WITH YOUR MOST
GENEROUS AFFECTIONS,
I DRIFT INTO A SLUMBER OF AWE UNTIL
YOU WAKE ME YET AGAIN WITH YOUR
MORNING
GLORY,
I GLADLY DRY YOUR FEET WITH MY HAIR,
ALWAYS YOUR HUMBLE SERVANT,
YOUR MODERN DAY MARY MADELINE.......

LONI ROSS

Grown Folks

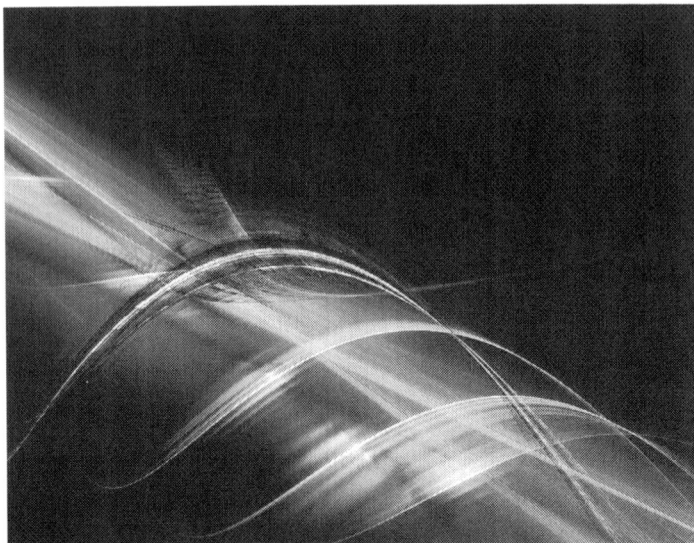

Willow...... SD Howard

Looking at you in your
state of glee, Profound and
pronounced is your tranquility.
Deeply rooted in your conviction
not once ever complaining about
your affection, defined are
your limbs, and the specific
meanings that they have for us.

Taking in the essence of your
being; slightly meaningful is
the way you sway, contained are
my feelings. Weep not on me.
Never leave me is my plea.
Guard my body continuously.
Far in the distance is the
end; I see you standing tall.
Never missing a beat, even
when your leaves fall.

Strong in stature and
rugged and unique, Everyone
love your appearance when
your blooms are at their peak.
The innocence of a child for
it is shelter that they seek.
Your vision has no appeal,
but your base just makes it
REAL!!!!!!

Stand tall, don't fall
remind us all, you're over all.
"Weep No More Willow"

Enlightened

I know I've been enlighten
I see thing so much clearer
Knowing knowing knowing
Learning understanding mind expanding
Midas touch I am the treasure
God just keeps getting better and better
Difficulty decease enjoying the ease
Please and at peace
Family and friends come around again
Love supersedes no longer offends
Like a messenger I see
Love is the key
God is so clever
Life is so much better
I once was blind but now I see
Thank God for enlighten me

KB

The Reality of if All….. by SD Howard

Emotions come and go,
but the spirit of my heart
you are truly the only one
that knows.

Running from your touch
on a regular basis, only
to find out that I was
coming in first in all the
wrong races.

My story is filled with all
the stories of what you've
done for me, but what will
the be able to say at the
end of my time, about what
I did for Thee.

I'm on bended knees to ask
that you recieve, because
before I was touched by
Your mighty word, I had
not achieved.......

Dear Heavenly Father, allow
me to embrace your word and
pass on what it means to me
to all that will read a work.....

Thank You.......in advance

IN A DARK PLACE

*I'VE TRIED AND TRIED TO DISTANCE MYSELF
FROM THE NONSENSE,*

*THE BULL AND OTHER SUCH ISSUES THAT HAVE
BECOME TRUELY A WASTE OF MY ENERGY AND
TIME.*

*THESE DAYS I FEEL LIKE I'M ON THE RUN FROM
MOMENTS THAT STAY TRYING TO BREAK ME
DOWN.*

*MY SHINE ONCE BLINDING, HOTTER THAN JULY,
NOW FADE AWAY GRAY LIKE A CLOUDY DAY IN
MAINE.*

MY SWAGGER, ONCE MY ATTENTION GRABBER,

*NOW A THING OF THE PAST AS MY DOWNWARD
GLANCES, MY BOWED SHOULDERS AND BACK
TEND TO GREET ONE'S FEET AS OPPOSED TO
THEIR FACE.*

*WHAT I PERCIEVE AS THE REAL HAS LATELY BEEN
CLOUDED CONSTANTLY BY RELATIONSHIP
GRIPES OF OLD AND NEW,*

INNER TURMOILS,

*DAY TO DAY TRIALS THAT KEEP MY BODY AND
SOUL IN A NEVERENDING UPROAR.*

*INSTEAD OF ME BEING FOCUSED AND ON MY
TOES,*

Grown Folks

I TEETER CONFUSED AND OFF BALANCED ON MY HEELS.

WHO KNOWS HOW IT FEELS WHEN YOUR EXHALES BECOME HARDER TO DISCHARGE SINCE THAT DEEP CLEANSING INHALE WHICH IS SUPPOSED TO ENFOLD ME IN BLISS HAS BECOME LIKE SMALL ARTICLES OF GLASS SLICING AWAY AT THE WRIST OF THE LITTLE GIRL THAT HIDES WITHIN.

MY FEELINGS THESE DAYS HAVE HELD ME CAPTIVE BECAUSE I HAVE CHOSEN TO CARE.

BECAUSE I HAVE DECIDED TO ACTUALLY BECOME MY BROTHER'S KEEPER AND WALKED A MILE IN HIS SHOES AND INSTEAD OF ACCOLADE I GET TO FEEL FIRST HAND,

HIS PAIN, HER FEARS, THEIR TEARS.
BUT IN DOING THIS SIMPLE ACT,
I'VE TURNED THE TABLES ON ME,
AND FOR SOME INSANE REASON I FEEL LIKE I CAN BREATH.
NOT SURE IF IT HAD ANYTHING TO DO WITH SHOULDERING SOME OF HIS DISPAIR,

DRINKING IN THE WINE OF HIS WHINE OR JUST GIVING HIM MY TIME.

EITHER WAY MY LIFE NOW SEEMS LIGHTER YET I'M NOT SURE HOW I CAN SMILE IN THE FACE OF MY FELLOW MAN'S PAIN.

LONI ROSS

Burnt Paper Note... ... by SD Howard

The place I'm in right now is very dark, I can see visions of me wrapping my hands around your neck and pushin outta you all the negative energy that binds you. I can't believe I ever loved you. What was it that I saw in you? I think to myself could it have ever been true.... Amazingly I just want this thing to go away and curse you for all the things that you have done. How could, you put your feelings before theirs, they didn't ask to be in this situation or for you do drop out of your mediation.... I'm really trying to stay focused and stop the insinuation about it was I ever saw in you. Did I think you were worthy of my seed and even the thought that you would keep my heart from ever being in need of the touch from another.... No, I was a fool for ever thinking that things could have ever worked out.... Yeah you gave me what God had purposed for me but that was His plan....

I was so out of it for this one but my feelings were on my sleeve and I just had to put it out of my head........

The Voice

As far back as I can remember, expressing myself has always been easier through someone else,
Learned behavior and feelings, things I never really knew, what I once lost I thought was gone for good,
Never missing it because I never knew it was mine, and as I grew I realize how much was really absent,
Instead of going forward I was at a standstill watching everyone else's progress, the way of life for me wasn't different, but very normal,
Going in circles, picking up and holding in my arms all that I could, never being able to put it in its rightful place and eventually dropping it all together waiting on another chance to go around the circle again,
Most of all I lost my voice, the only thing that could keep me alive, it fell so far down inside me and then imbedded itself in my flesh, like a limb or an extra organ, not belonging,
But something happened and my voice wouldn't leave me alone, started telling my secrets, reminding me of the power in speaking up and out against those who wanted to remove my sound box that added volume to a once soundless voice,
Bound by the fear and anger that held my voice down, turned down so low until I thought that it was nonexistent,

But I have a voice and I have a choice to speak out and up, not thinking about the embarrassment to come from ones sheepish scam, with threatening looks and piercing stairs,

After stealing and robbing the voice out of me, the one thing I have to set me free, allowing me to be me, I can talk to myself, the words surface from the prison its known, they are true and blossom as they are spoken, convincing myself of who I really am, I now can pay attention to how different I am,

My nose, my thighs and my toes, living in the one safe place I know, my head; having the courage to go down where my voice use to dwell and visit who I am, to see my legs and the dimples in my knees, the lifeline on my stomach and my private place,

They all make up me, my voice and me have made me free, and it lives inside of me this being created perfect as can be,

No longer have I to wait for someone to sort through my crying and moaning and tears to convince me of what I'm trying to say,

I have a voice and I can tell it like no one else, my voice in me…

Linda hart – Washington

Grown Folks

Yes We Can

This message is to all current and future teachers.
It is my honor to offer encouraging words of
wisdom.
I'll guide the future teachers from all higher
learning institutes
to bridge gaps in education whatever that may
constitute.
We've reviewed ideas that have worked
we've seen programs that don't.
It's our job to keep researching
because teaching is hard work.
This is a profession fueled by passion and is hard
if you're introvert. Connect with all of your
students
to keep them on a lighter note.
Identify with all in every way possible.
They say don't get too close
to your students but in reality that's impossible.
If we never make connections
How will we be mentioned as honorable?
The youth are our future, there's no doubt about it
so from present and so forth
we must encourage those who need guidance,
and if there are any on the wrong track
we must learn how to reroute them,

and properly equip ourselves
with extended amounts of knowledge,
in every subject possible
even after we've left college.
Many problems will arise many diversities will
come to light.
Many obstacles we must override, that may not be
in plain sight.
We must stay optimistic because armed with
knowledge we will all fight.
The gaps will be bridged...but of course not
overnight
but stand together stand tall educators from big
too small.
United we will stand hoping that we never fall.
We will push students to spring even if it's only
Fall.
United We Will Stand because we've decided not
to fall
YES WE CAN! NOW LET ME HEAR IT FROM
YOU ALL!
"YES WE CAN!" (Chants) with an audience
applause.

- Aaron Smith aka Poetic NJustice

Turning The Page... ... by SD Howard

My chest is full of emotion, my head full of devotion. Heaven has manifested itself in my inner most thoughts. My mind wonders often as to what my place is. Surely it will come to pass that I know what my place is.

My heart is heavy with thoughts of failure and regret, but all in all I see how I think He would want me to pay my debt. Shall I say it, or will He allow me to make it.

My father is a just father and He gives me just what I need, just when I need it. My cup run-ith over several times with blessings and I've looked the other way, today is much different and I need Him in the worst way. Begging & pleading is never what to do but as long as you follow and trust in the Lord He will always be there for you.

Love, Peace and Serenity

Love peace and serenity never hate your enemy
if you stand for nothing you will fall for anything
if you're in my vicinity than you are now a friend
to me
even if you're far away just twitter mention me
your soul lasts until infinity
while your body is a temporary home rented by
your entity
hate fuels a cold world love is warm like humidity
daunting tasks can be quenched providing energy
as long as there are oceans close in the vicinity
my passion will increase as my pen leaks with
more intensity
the whole earth is my home so homelessness can
never enter me
my body is my temple and my soul shares its
empathy
they say love is hard to find but to me it's getting
clearer
you can never find true Love until you find it in
the mirror
cause in reality that guy cupid could never help
Love is only hard to find if you don't look within
yourself

- Aaron Smith aka Poetic NJustice

6 THEM

Yo Game Ain't Tight…….. SD Howard

Outstretched arms I have,
wanting you to accept me.
Don't allow me to disappear
into obscurity, come up and save me.
Help me to be the person that
you want me to be.
Mold me, without trying to
control me. Praise me, without
that silly ass grin trying
to degrade me. If I know anything it's
that I won't allow you to make me
feel like less than what I am.
You can't hurt me with your idle
thoughts. Release me from your mental
jail, without my love you can go to hell.
You've hurt me for long enough. Now it's
time to feel another's touch. Touch my hand,
make me aware that you are there. Touch my
cheeks and watch the rise you get from my
twinpeaks. Come to me and speak in words that
will allow me to understand that you want
only me.

You continue to make advances at me
yet I see your ass walking round with the
hand of another. Should I believe you
or should I relieve you, of the bullshit
that you're pedalin'.

Blame

To whom do we place blame?
When I can see this vivid picture as i see sick
growing sea sick from crime waves
big enough to bury the titanic, no lives saved
phony KONY antics got me frantic as crime waves
but I never wave back I just watch as time pays
We living in our last days
but how can we think about progression when we
lost in a daze?
Racism is less direct but black hatred is still blatant
I refuse to be a paraplegic within your races
give a black child a skin color to choose he'll
switch races
because the brain washed up thoughts that show
how T.V. raised him
made him feel insignificant and the ignorance just
fuels it
cause the role models that interest them push
crack and resembles men
and through the music, they're fed foolishness,
given steps how to use a clip and shoot a 5th
until news clips show more of them getting cuffed
rather than schooling them
and as we follow wicked ways we realize it is the
fool in him
but how can we continue on this path with many
dead ends
and wrong turns and blocked lens from
consciousness

I'm not content with all of this
we're trying to find who to blame so call the devil
white men
but for every erect index there's ten pointing
opposite
like YOU know YOU shouldn't drink, cause you
don't know your own tolerance
so who's the blame now but the idiot who bought
the shit?
We chose to blame the U.S. but U.S. stands for us,
so I've flipped that acronym
cause we will never make progress until we
choose to Speak Up!

Aaron Smith aka Poetic NJustice

They was laffin at me, so I began to cry,
Not because they hurt me inside,
Not because of my foolish pride,
But simply because they could not see how beautiful I
was inside.
They could not see that I was to be a stunning
Mother,
Cousin,
Lover,
Friend,
Homemaker,
Sister,
Champion of their causes when all hope was lost.
They didn't have a clue,
That I could build too,
I could invent,
I could discover,
I could create from dirt,
I could change the world,
I could impregnate young minds with wisdom,
I could smother their doubts with devotion.
But All they could see was that I was..
Black,
I had ashy knees,
I had hair texture like wool,
I was poor,
I was a female,
I was a child,
I was stupid,
I was going nowhere
Because to them I was simply nobody.
And to me, I cried because as long as they were blind....
It was them who would be forever nobody too.
LONI ROSS

I See You.... Lookin   by SD Howard

Mental misfits have no place with me

I'm sure there's an audience but it ain't clear to me

Sometimes we wanna let our manhood show

but then we have to remember our shit didn't grow.

Fuck around and get in a bag you can't break

I ain't never be one to play around like a fake.

Let's hope that fayo sake.....

You done just made a mistake

Thought you came up on a soft ass dude....

That's far from the truth and these words do bruise

Several times you wannapatcho chest

Then you think about that extra flesh...

It's clear to me that you feel the need to show ya teeth

When U getcho beast mode up come thru and

lemme see

Childhood pranks and games ain't a thing to me

But the next time let's see if we can collect a fee.

A King's thrown is the place to be....

I don't think I need to claim it to see

All the simple pleasures that U plan to be...

Grave diggin seems to suit you...

Lemme take a seat while you Do U...

WHAT YOU MEAN TO ME...DEDICATED TO
THE MEN, LOST AND FOUND

THE MUFASA TO MY SARABI,
THE GREAT WHITE TO MY ORCA,
THE SHAKA TO MY NATION,
THE DELIVERANCE TO MY FREEDOM.

I STAND HUMBLY AT THE FOOT OF HIS
THRONE,
CASTING AWAY ALL THOUGHTS OF DOUBT
AS EACH DAY I WATCH YOU WALK
PROUDLY AMONG THE CONCRETE CLOUDS.
BUT A BIT OF SADNESS DOES CREEP INTO MY
SOUL,
FOR YOU ARE MOST WANTED,
MOST FEARED,
NUMBER ONE SPECIES MOST HUNTED AND
WHY?
JUST BECAUSE OF YOUR BIRTHRIGHT.

NEVER MATTER,
HEAD HELD HIGH, STRUT OXEN STRONG,
APPEASING GOD BY MODELING HIS MOST
MAGNIFICANT CREATION.
ATTITUDE THAT MYSTIFIES ALL,
SKIN KISSED BY THE SUN,
3 SHADES OF DARKNESS, BLACK, BLACKER
AND BLUE,
OR
BUTTER PECAN DELIGHT.

NO MATTER THE PERSUASION,
IT'S ABOUT WHAT SLAVING IN THE FIELDS
HAS FORCED YOU TO BRING TO THE TABLE,
A MOUSE OR A MAN!!!!!

CALLOUSES HARD LIKE FORGOTTEN WORLD
WAR COINS,
BACK BENT FROM YEARS OF WEATHERING
ALL STORMS,
BUT STILL YOU RISE TO THE OCCASION
WHENEVER CALLED UPON TO HELP
PRODUCE AND TEACH A NEW GENERATION
THE IMPORTANCE OF WALKING TALL,
NEVER LET THEM SEE YOU FALL.

FRAIL TO THE SYSTEM,
I THINK NOT,
IT IS THE SYSTEM THAT COWERS BEFORE
YOU SO MUCH SO THAT IT MUST FIGHT THE
DIRTY FIGHT TO KEEP YOU DOWN AND OUT.

BUT YOU ARE ALL ABOUT 360 DEGREES
ANGLE,
EVER CHANGING,
EVER EVOLVING,
EVER EDUCATING
ILLUMINATING,
SOARING,
LEADING
AND DEVOURING ALL WHO PROTEST.

AND IN I MY INFINITE WISDOM,

I SIT BACK IN MY ROCKING CHAIR AND
WATCH AND BE HONORED,
FOR I HAVE BORN UNTO THIS HERE WORLD A
PRINCE,
AND ON MY KNEES I CONSTANTLY THANK
THEE,
GRACIOUS TO GOD IS WHAT I BE,
FOR IN ME,
I WAS BLESSED TO HARBOR THE SEED OF A....

KING!

LONI ROSS

She Stayed...... SD Howard

I'm in a mood and there is nothing that you can do
I want you to just back up and walk away but you
won't so for that I'm gonna open up my bag and
blast yo ass with everything that I have. I have let
you get away with all that you've done for years
but today you fucked up and caused me to have an
abundance of tears... Yeah, don't fear cause these
gun blast won't stray and when they hit your ass
they won't fray anything but that skin from your
bone and leave that ass shattered and alone, just like
you did me, in my dreams what did it mean, to you.
Did you think this was just something to do are did
it really mean something to you. You thought I was
lame and didn't have a thought of this time frame
that you tried to get me to go along with but you
forget that I'm a real man and one that doesn't fall
victim to these silly ass game that you continue to
try to play, I was all a part of the bigger picture
and you were never even a small ass figure but I
allowed you to stay and what a day you got me and
I had nothing to say but she stayed..........

Now What.......

AFRIKA

See I used to be a nigga before I went to school.
now I have knowledge that the nobles use to use.
A stands for
anybody that acknowledges their roots
and the truth you not just a little nigga turned
loose
you're a noble Black King
that should be spiritually attuned
but instead you're in your room
learning from movies songs and news.
new and inventive ways on how to become a goon
F stands for
anybody that forgives but won't forget
R is a
reminder that civility is a gift
because without the ancient KMT civilization
would not exist
I is for Isis for
she's the Goddess of Heaven
K is for King, every
Kingdom is a blessing
and **A** is for
anybody that acknowledges their roots
and the truth you not just a little nigga turned
loose

you're a noble Black King that should be
spiritually attuned
When I'm dead when I'm ghost
Will you remember me as a nigga or a brotha with
hope?
You can brush this off as one but God ain't no
joke.
Next time put your face in a book,
instead of face booking for pokes
while searching Google for new status update
quotes.

-AARON SMITH AKA POETIC NJUSTICE

ABOUT THE AUTHORS

Loni Ross – Is every women it's all in her, she is an exceptional mother and a Office Manager of Dental Office on Wall Street in New York City. Making it there and with her talented writing style she is giving it to us everywhere around the world.

Linda Hart- Washington – an Office Manager at a Medical Research Facility in Gaithersburg, MD. Linda has been in this particular field for over twelve years. Starting out as a Customer Service Representative and working her way up to Office Manager. After a few hardships and having to move, turning a 3 mile commute each way into a 50 mile commute each way really didn't leave a lot of time to put her thoughts down on paper. She's back to her 3 mile commute again and living in Gaithersburg, MD with her two children and daughters Pomeranian, Sweetie doing what she loves most. This will be her first

Aaron Smith aka Poetic NJustice – spent half of his life in Germantown, MD and the other half in Washington, DC. He's currently studying at Bowie State University as a creative writing major and a child and adolescent studies minor. Aaron is 20 years old and aspires to be a world renowned poet and author. He is truly a visionary, optimist, and monotheist. Follow him on twitter: @Poetic_Njustice

Shelby D. Howard Jr. - A God fearing husband, father and grandfather who continue to look for ways to grow in an effort to move forward. D.O.B: September 18, 1973, born and raised in East St. Louis, IL. He moved from there to Cahokia, IL at 13. Writing material since age 12 but never really thought seriously about getting anything published of his own but he did. Shelby's first book of poems and short stories is titled. " A Confused Mind With Simple Thoughts" He look forward to many more. He is a motivating, mind stimulating artist using writing as a means to convey a message to those that will accept it.

Kimberly Frazier Burkley -Neptune

I am the 8th planet from the sun, in Rome they
don't know me. In Greek Mythology lays my
history, in this life as he was I am the God of the
sea. So I made her emotional just like me, with
some violent tendencies.

Scars from being swallowed at birth I pick my
brother here on earth to save me again from
Cronus who is now my Rhea. Rhea is now Cronus
cousin… oh how history repeats…
I am the fourth largest planet by diameter, but still
waters run deep

Zeus, my soter what has happened to you, oh how
I weep… Strike the Titans! The strength is in you
as in me. Once again overpower Cronus and that
spirit of jealousy. Zeus your Cronus is your Rhea
she can't set you free Confusing holding on to
dreams and nightmares of history

Circus Flaminius, Campus Martius my powers of
Stallions running free. Instead they named U.S.
ballistic missile after me… My heart sinks, so I
gave birth to tsunami, Katrina, Sandy most
recently. Pain so great the earth will shake crack
and bleed.

As you'll have me believe in the trinity I must
conceive that now I am the sea. Poseidon is to the
sea as God is to Jesus. I once was a God

Made in the USA
Lexington, KY
01 February 2013